The Battle of
Losecoat Field
1470

Rupert Matthews

Essex County Council

Acknowledgements
Photos, illustrations and maps are by the author except:
Gainsborough Hall Asterion;
Drawings by Leanne Goodall and Darren Bennett.

Website - www.BretwaldaBooks.com
Twitter - @Bretwaldabooks
Facebook - Bretwalda Books
Blog - bretwaldabooks.blogspot.co.uk/

First Published 2013
Text Copyright © Rupert Matthews 2013
Photos, maps and illustrations Copyright © Rupert Matthews 2013, unless otherwise stated
Rupert Matthews asserts his moral rights to be regarded as the author of this work.
All rights reserved. No reproduction of any part of this publication
is permitted without the prior written permission of the publisher:

Bretwalda Books
Unit 8, Fir Tree Close, Epsom,
Surrey KT17 3LD
info@BretwaldaBooks.com
www.BretwaldaBooks.com
ISBN 978-1-909099-66-1

Contents

Introduction 4
Chapter 1 The Wars of the Roses 5
Chapter 2 Men, Weapons and Tactics 14
Chapter 3 The Battle of Losecoat Field 30
Chapter 4 Aftermath 46

The Battle of Losecoat Field 1470

INTRODUCTION

Empingham is today a quiet, pleasant little village astride the A606 next to the artificial reservoir of Rutland Water. The stone-built village clusters around the crossroads of Main Street and Church Street. Today the A606 carries traffic from Stamford to Uppingham just outside the village thanks to a 20th century slip road. It might be difficult to imagine a more tranquil or relaxing spot. Certainly sipping an ale in the garden of the White Horse pub and listening to the birdsong over the distant hum of traffic is a pleasant enough experience.

But appearances can be deceptive, for this area of gentle English countryside was once the scene of slaughter, bloodshed and violence on a grand scale. The Battle of Empingham, or Losecoat Field, was fought just outside the village to the northeast at a spot now known as Bloody Oaks - an ominous name that was gained for grim reasons.

The battle fought here was waged as part of the Wars of the Roses that tore England apart in a struggle as vicious and deadly as any war ever fought. The heraldry of the knights in armour may have been colourful and bright, but the edges of their swords were wickedly sharp and the war was fought with a merciless savagery that England has rarely seen before or since.

Not only that but the conflict that took place here saw one of the first appearances on the battlefield in England of artillery. Guns were not exactly new in 1470, but they had until recently been big, cumbersome objects used in sieges. Now lighter guns were becoming available that could be trundled around a field with relative ease - and they were put to murderous use at Empingham.

And yet Empingham was not a straightforward battle. This was no set piece conflict of York vs Lancaster. Instead the battle was the result of plotting, treason and subterfuge such that nobody could be entirely certain of whose side other men were really on.

It was King Edward IV of England who fought here. And it was he who had to contend with treachery and rebellion, replying with the heroism, dash and skill that were to make him one of the most feared commanders of the medieval period.

Chapter 1
The Wars of the Roses

The Wars of the Roses were fought with a curious mix of merciless savagery and almost considerate care that has not been seen in wars in Britain either before of since. The struggle tore England apart between 1455 and 1497, with the Battle of Losecoat Field, or Empingham, displaying both heartless, almost casual violence alongside a regard for humanity as strongly as any other battle during these terrible wars.

The peculiar character of the wars can be traced back to the reasons they were fought and the characters of those involved. Although some historians have looked for underlying social trends or economic factors behind the Wars of the Roses, they remained at heart a dynastic battle fought for political power between the two main branches of the Plantagenet dynasty that had ruled England since 1154. It was ironic that the great struggle between the two would result in an entirely different dynasty taking the crown in the shape of the Tudors.

The foundations for the struggle were laid in 1399 when Richard II was overthrown by his cousin Henry Bolingbroke, who became Henry IV. Richard II had proved to be a weak king and a petulant and spiteful man. He raised taxes to pay for his luxurious lifestyle, then executed those who objected. The final straw came when John of Gaunt, Duke of Lancaster died. Gaunt's eldest son, Henry Bolingbroke, had already been sent into exile by Richard on trumped up charges. Now Richard announced that the entire, vast Lancaster estates were confiscated by the crown.

Bolingbroke was furious, but he was also very popular among both the nobles and commons of England. On 4 July Bolingbroke landed in Yorkshire declaring that he had come to reclaim his rightful inheritance and to reform the evil government of England. Men flocked to his banner, even royal castles throwing their gates open, and nobody supported Richard at all. What made Bolingbroke's arrival dangerous was that he, like Richard, was a grandson of King Edward III. Before long Richard was in prison and Bolingbroke was being hailed as King

The Battle of Losecoat Field 1470

Henry IV. Richard died conveniently soon after and since he had no children, Henry IV was secure on the throne.

Almost unnoticed at the time was a great grandson of Edward III. This was Edmund Mortimer, Earl of March, who was just 8 years old. By the rules of inheritance at the time, it was Edmund who should have become king when Richard II died, but being so young, Edmund was ignored by everyone involved and, indeed, was seen to support the new King Henry IV. Richard had been the son of Edward III's eldest son, another Edward. Henry of Bolingbroke was son of Edward III's third son. Edmund was the son of Philippa, daughter of Lionel Duke of Clarence who was Edward III's second son.

Henry IV proved to be an effective and popular monarch, as did his son, Henry V. During these years neither Edmund nor his children made any claim on the throne and the kingdom was content and peaceful. The trouble flared when Henry V's son became king as Henry VI. The new king proved to be a weak man who was easily influenced by those around him. He gained a reputation for piety and gentleness, but his government grew progressively worse. Henry's queen, Margaret of Anjou, was a grasping and scheming lady who surrounded herself with clever but amoral men intent on milking the state treasury for their own benefit. At first they moved carefully, but by the later 1440s they had secured a grip on power that enabled them to buy and sell offices, pursue private feuds and largely ignore the laws of England by bribing or intimidating judges.

Those opposed to Margaret and her henchmen gathered around Richard, Duke of York. At this date York was in France fighting the later stages of the Hundred Year's War against France. Although hampered by the lack of money, men and supplies that he needed - the money going into the pockets of Margaret and her cronies - he was holding his own and even won the Battle of Fecamp. Of more relevance to events in England was the fact that York governed the extensive English lands in France with honesty, fairness and efficiency. Contrasted with the mess at home in England, York's government was a shining example.

Hoping to take the shine off York's achievements Margaret of Anjou sent out her ally the Duke of Somerset with a beautifully equipped army and orders to attack the French. Somerset's campaign proved to be a costly failure as he proved to be as inept at war as he was at government. Margaret was furious with York for his success and persuaded King Henry to withdraw him from France. York was too dangerous to keep in England so he was packed off to Ireland with a ten year appointment to administer the royal lands there. York returned to England occasionally to attend meetings of the Royal Council, but was invariably snubbed and ignored.

Then in 1453 King Henry VI fell into a stupor. At the time it was said that he had gone mad, but it would now seem that he suffered some form of major mental breakdown that left him unable to respond or react to what went on around him. Noblemen opposed to Margaret of Anjou clamoured for York to be brought back from Ireland and made Regent of the Kingdom during the King's madness. Among these emerging Yorkists was the Richard Neville, Earl of Warwick, perhaps the richest man in England after the king and a dashingly handsome young man with an emerging reputation as a talented military commander. York came to England, took the title of Lord Protector and began ruling England. His regime soon proved to be every bit as efficient and honest as had his rule in France.

Then in 1455 Henry recovered his senses. The Council of Regency was disbanded and Margaret and Somerset put back into office. It was at this point that a famous incident is supposed to have taken place, though contemporary evidence for it is lacking. A large group of nobles was taking the air in the gardens of the Temple Church in the city of London during a court meeting when York entered through one gate and Somerset a few seconds later by way of another. York then picked a white rose from a bush in the garden, the white rose being a heraldic badge associated with his family. Somerset promptly picked a red rose from a different bush. Warwick then picked a white rose, followed by nobles supporting York, while those backing Somerset hurried to pick red roses and those unwilling to commit themselves in so obviously a dangerous dispute rushed to get out of the garden.

What made York all the more dangerous to Margaret, Somerset and their supporters was the fact that he was the grandson of Edmund Mortimer, the boy who had been passed over when Henry IV became king. In strict legal terms, York should have been king, not Henry. Neither York nor his supporters pushed this claim, but everyone knew about it and it lurked in the background of all these events.

The Duke of Somerset and Margaret summoned a Great Council to meet in Leicester in May 1455, apparently with the aim of arresting Warwick and other supporters of York on trumped up charges of treason. York decided to attend, hastily gathering a force of armed retainers to ensure his safety. At St Albans on 22 May York and his men got engaged in a vicious and bloody fight with

The Battle of Losecoat Field 1470

Somerset's men. Somerset and his friend Henry Percy, Earl of Northumberland, were both killed. Later historians dubbed this the First Battle of St Albans, though in truth it was more a nasty scuffle with edged weapons that ended with the deaths of only around 40 of the 5,000 men present.

York now returned to government, but he sought to mend fences with his opponents, recognising that many of them had opposed him out of loyalty to King Henry. Nevertheless, the bloodshed at St Albans had shown that violence and armies could be used to solve political problems. With England resembling an armed camp due to the need to support the wars in France, there were large

King Edward IV was the commander of the royal army at the Battle of Losecoat Field, the only battle ever fought in Rutland. He was marching north to deal with a rebellion in Lincolnshire when he unexpectedly met the main force of rebels just north of Stamford.

numbers of soldiers and commanders around. Margaret with the Dukes of Suffolk and Somerset smiled at York and Warwick, but in fact were preparing for an armed struggle. They spread all sorts of accusations about York, drummed up loyalty to the anointed king and in October 1459 they struck. At Ludford Bridge in Shropshire York was caught by Margaret and Henry with a superior force. York's men refused to fight against an army led by King Henry, so York fled to Ireland with his eldest son Edmund, Earl of Rutland, to escape the deaths he knew Margaret had planned for them. Warwick likewise went abroad taking with him York's second son Edward, Earl of March.

However, many in England did not want Margaret, Suffolk and their supporters to have untrammelled power and appeals went to York to return. Early in 1460 York, Rutland, March and Warwick returned to England. Men flocked to their banners. At Northampton Warwick and March crushed the main Lancastrian army. Henry was recognised as king, but York was appointed his successor. That angered Margaret of Anjou who saw her son, Edward, being excluded from the crown that she saw as rightfully his. Her men ambushed and killed York at Wakefield. Rutland was caught and murdered soon after.

Warwick and young Edward - now Duke of York - began gathering an army in London. Edward now openly claimed the crown through his descent from Edmund Mortimer. At the Battle of Towton on 29 March 1461 Edward and Warwick utterly defeated the supporters of Margaret and Henry. The Lancastrian leaders were killed, Henry captured and put under house arrest, while Margaret was driven into exile with her son Edward. Edward of York was crowned King Edward IV and soon proved himself to be as capable and honest as his father. It appeared to all that the Wars of the Roses were over. Edward had won and become reconciled to all but his most intransigent enemies. England settled down to peace, but it was a peace that was not to last forever.

The unexpected source of future bloodshed when it came was the Earl of Warwick, that staunchest and most talented support of first the Duke of York and then of Edward IV. As the years passed, Warwick began to believe two dangerous things. First he became convinced that it was his skills and popularity that had put Edward on the throne, and second he believed that he was being inadequately thanked for his efforts. Undoubtedly Warwick had played a major part in Edward's success, but it had not been him alone. First York and then Edward had been popular and talented in their own right, while the incompetence of Henry's government had driven many to support the Yorkists.

The Battle of Losecoat Field 1470

Warwick's anger was increased by Edward's odd choice of wife. Edward was tall, good looking and charming. From his teenage years he had gained a reputation as a ladies man and there were numerous and frequent rumours and gossip about affairs with both single and married women. Edward showed a liking for women from untitled families and several London merchants had reason to suspect why the king called on them so often. None of these romances appeared to be serious, nor long lasting. Warwick and most other nobles viewed them as the indulgences of a handsome young man without a father's restraining hand upon him. Now that Edward was king, serious talks began about finding him a

A 19th century imagining of Elizabeth Woodville. Undoubtedly beautiful and intelligent, Elizabeth proved to be a poor choice as queen for Edward IV. Her relatives were greedy and grasping, managing to upset the proud Earl of Warwick who gradually turned against Edward IV. The Battle of Losecoat Field was one result of the growing enmity.

suitable wife. Diplomacy came first, of course, with Warwick playing a leading role in finding a foreign bride who would bring serious advantages to England.

But then rumours began to spread that Edward had got married in secret to one of his lovers. Warwick refused to believe it, but it was true. Edward had married Elizabeth Woodville. Everyone could see Elizabeth's attraction for Edward as a mistress - she was young, beautiful and intelligent - but as a queen she was a bizarre choice. She was a commoner and the widow of a Lancastrian knight who had been killed fighting against Edward himself. Warwick was furious, believing that Edward had given way to lust over the duties of a king.

And so by 1467 Warwick was a disgruntled man. Also peeved was George, Duke of Clarence. Clarence was Edward's younger brother. He had been only a child during the fighting and had taken no part. He was now 18 years old and had grown to be resentful of his elder brother's success, charm and popularity. Clarence wanted honours and money, but no matter how much Edward gave him Clarence was never satisfied. Whenever a rich estate became available, Clarence wanted it. Edward, of course, had to hand out honours, positions and money to other noblemen to build alliances and show favour in return for work done for the kingdom. Clarence did not recognise this and resented every gift that went to another. Clarence's disaffection may have been made all the worse by the hero-worship shown toward Edward by the youngest of the three brothers, Richard Duke of Gloucester who was then aged 15.

In 1466 Warwick let it be known that he was looking for a husband for his eldest daughter and main heiress, Isabel. Richard of Gloucester may have been young, but he was already spending a lot of time with Warwick's younger daughter Anne and a romance between the two was rumoured. Perhaps for this reason Clarence decided he wanted to marry Isabel. This was a serious problem for Edward. If both his brothers married daughters of Warwick it would make the disgruntled earl dangerously powerful and influential. Edward summoned his brothers and made them promise not to marry without his permission. Richard agreed, Clarence did so only under protest.

In July 1469 Clarence married Isabel without permission. Edward woke up to be told the news by armed men sent by Warwick. Edward may have feared for his life, and there is good reason to believe that Warwick intended that Edward should meet with an unfortunate accident so that Clarence would become king. Certainly two of Elizabeth Woodville's relatives were killed on Warwick's orders. But very quickly the people of England made their views known. Noble after noble sent messages to Edward declaring their loyalty while town and city councils passed resolutions declaring their love and affection for their sovereign Edward.

Warwick was no fool. He realised that he would not live long if Edward were to die, so instead he protested his own loyalty and explained he had acted out of affection for the king and for England. If only a few grievances were settled, Warwick said, he would be happy. During tense talks at Warwick's powerful Middleham Castle, Edward gave Warwick everything he wanted and then ostentatiously called for his horse as he said he wanted to go to London. Warwick made no move to stop him, so Edward rode free.

On the surface it appeared that England was still a peaceful nation. Clarence was happily married to a rich and good looking girl, Warwick was enjoying his vast wealth and luxurious lifestyle while Edward was in London ruling as King of England.

It is difficult at this distance in time to know how secure or fragile was the agreement between Edward and Warwick. It may be that Warwick had learned his lesson, and Edward was content to have humbled the earl. On the other hand it may be that both men were secretly plotting the other's downfall. Nor is it entirely clear what Clarence's views were. If he had for a few weeks thought he would soon be king, that ambition may have remained.

What we do know is what happened next. And it was a trail of events that was to end in bloody violence near Empingham in Rutland.

Facing page: Edward IV hurriedly leaves Middleham Castle as a feast takes place to escape the Earl of Warwick. The falling out between King Edward and his most fervent supporter was to have devastating repercussions that would plunge England into civil war.

The Battle of Losecoat Field 1470

Chapter 3
Men, Weapons and Tactics

The armies of the Wars of the Roses were raised in three basic ways. First there were the town and county militias, second were the retainers of the various noblemen and third were mercenaries, mostly foreigners. The size of the armies involved has provoked a lot of dispute. Contemporary chroniclers had not, by and large, been anywhere near the fighting since most of them were monks or clerics. They recorded figures of anything between 20,000 and 80,000 men for the armies involved, but this was probably based more on guesswork than anything else. Modern historians have tended to reduce these numbers substantially, suggesting that most armies were around 10,000 to 15,000 strong with the largest army fielded at this date being the 35,000 Lancastrians who fought at Towton in 1461. However, it must be said that these historians are working on little more than guesswork as well. The only firm information we have comes in scraps here and there, such as the fact that in 1454 the Duke of Buckingham paid for 2,000 badges to be sewn on the cloaks of his men going to patrol the Scottish Border or that in 1455 Coventry town council bought 100 suits of clothes for the citizens who were serving in the militia that year. It is likely that in the earlier phases of the war the armies were larger than later on, though what the number at any particular battle may have been it is impossible to know for certain.

The town and county militias in the 15th century were the descendants of the old feudal levy. This had stated that every able-bodied man aged 16 to 60 had to be ready to defend his local town or county in times of war. The first 40 days was unpaid and compulsory, but after that the men had to be paid and had to volunteer to serve. It had been so long since England had been invaded by anyone that the original system had fallen into disuse. Instead it had evolved into a way of raising a semi-professional force of men for longer periods of time.

Each town and city was expected to have a full time guard which patrolled the city walls, secured the city gates at night and kept order on the streets. The men would also guard the gates during the day, collecting any tolls that were due from merchants and keeping an eye open for undesirables. These men might number only a dozen or so and were employed full time by the council, their equipment, food and lodging usually being provided.

There was also the militia, sometimes termed "trained bands", made up of citizens who were trained to use weapons at weekends, but who worked at their own trades during the week. Arrangements varied, but these men were usually paid a small amount each month in return for turning up to train equipped with weapons and armour. Each town or county employed a Constable who was responsible for training the men, checking their equipment and recording any absences from training sessions. In times of war he was the commander of the unit on campaign.

When a royal "commission of array" arrived asking for the militia to turn out it usually specified the numbers of men needed and how long they would serve for. It was then the task of the local authorities to find the men, usually volunteers from among those who came for training. While the men were usually expected to provide their own weapons and armour, it was the town council or county sheriff who paid and supplied their clothes and food out of local taxation. In most instances the men would be provided with a new suit of clothes and a travelling cloak before they set off. These clothes were provided in bulk by the authorities and while they fell short of being a uniform they did tend to be in a uniform colour or pattern which meant that all men from one town or county were dressed alike. Nottingham, for instance, is known to have supplied red outfits while Coventry favoured red and green stripes.

As for weapons, it would seem that the militia tended to go for weapons that did not demand much in the way of skill to wield in battle. In 1457 the men of Bridport, Dorset, paraded armed with a sword and dagger each, plus a shield, helmet and quilted jacket. The rural village of Ewelme in Oxfordshire provided a rather more mixed array. Among the 6 men recorded as parading for training were two archers, one of whom had a helmet and body armour, three men with partial armour and a bill and one man who had no armour and was armed with "a staff". Quite how much use the last would be in battle is unclear, though all armies needed someone to collect firewood and dig latrines so perhaps that was his task.

In normal conditions these militia did little fighting for they were not destined for overseas service in the French wars. Instead they were used for duties closer to home, manning coastal defences, castles and assorted strongpoints.

The Battle of Losecoat Field 1470

However, the years of the Wars of the Roses were not usual conditions. The militia were under the control of the crown and so were expected to be loyal to the reigning monarch. This was part of the military set up that for centuries had made England far less prone to rebellions and civil wars than other European states. With so much of the military apparatus in the hands of the monarch, it was a brave nobleman indeed who started an armed rebellion.

However, the Duke of York was not launching an armed rebellion against the king. He always made it very clear that he was loyal to King Henry VI, but was instead seeking to free the king from dishonest advisers. He therefore felt free to summon militias in the name of the king, as did Queen Margaret. This put the local authorities in something of a quandary. If they ignored a commission of array they might be charged with treason, while if they answered it they might be aiding a cause they did not support. Few records have survived to show how local authorities coped, but we know of the reaction of Norwich in 1461.

In the spring the city received a commission of array from Queen Margaret in the name of King Henry VI. The commission demanded 120 fully equiped infantry to fight against rebels and traitors. Norwich city council complied promptly enough, getting volunteers together, providing them with campaigning suits of clothes and checking over their arms and armour. But before the 120 men set off they held a meeting in front of the cathedral. After some discussion the men decided that they favoured the Yorkist cause, and so marched to fight against Margaret instead of for her. The council was, apparently, not consulted and the decision made by the men themselves.

We know that militias fought on both sides during the Wars of the Roses, but unlike the men of Norwich in 1461 we do not know how they decided which side to support.

If details of the militia are rather scarce, we know rather more about the retainers as this system involved cash changing hands for written contracts, called indentures, some of which have survived. The system began to develop under Edward III who needed a reliable supply of men willing to serve across the Channel in France.

By the time of Edward III in the mid-14th century the old feudal system had more or less broken down. Instead of knights and barons who held land from the crown paying for it by serving as an armed man when needed, it had become more normal for them to pay a tax known as scutage. This was, in theory, set at a rate that allowed the monarch to hire a mercenary to do the military service instead. However, Edward had found that foreign mercenaries were unreliable. Instead he gradually developed the indenture system.

Under this system the king gave a noble or knight a contract to provide a set number of armed men of various types for a specific period of time for a set rate of pay. The contracts generally ran for three months, six months or a year. Most were concerned with the summer campaigning season, while the annual contracts were for castle guard duty and patrolling frontiers. Because the indentures were usually renewed year after year, the men became effectively full time professional soldiers. Knowing that they would get paid for years, the men realised it was worth their while to invest in top quality equipment and put in the many hours of training needed to master the often complex skills of medieval warfare.

Rates of pay varied, but the average for the mid 15th century was for an archer to get three pennies a day, a hobilar six pennies, a man at arms one shilling, a knight two shillings a knight banneret four shillings and a nobleman six shillings and eight pennies. There was usually a "regard" paid at the end of the contract, assuming that the men had performed their duties well. This might be as much as the value of the contract, but was usually less. All pay was in cash and if the pay fell into arrears the men were entitled to go home before the contract ended.

This fully armoured knight wears the very latest and finest armour, so he must be a rich man. The body is entirely encased in plates of quality steel shaped to fit the individual. Pieces of mail are used to give added protection at joints. His main weapon is a poleaxe, with a long sword as a secondary weapon. This sort of armour was surprisingly light and flexible, allowing the wearer freedom of movement.

The Battle of Losecoat Field 1470

The ratios between the different types of man also varied, but by 1450 it was usual for there to be five or six archers for each man at arms, three or four men at arms for each knight (nobles counting as knights for this purpose). The size of indentures varied wildly with individual knights agreeing a contract to come along in person along with half a dozen archers, while the famous commanders might agree to provide up to 4,000 men. Interestingly the numbers of men a commander could put together bore no relation to his social rank. The Earl of Devon could muster only 110 men, while Sir Robert Knollys, a mere knight, could regularly field over 3,000 men. It was fame and competence that enabled a man to attract followers, not wealth or rank.

As a rule the same men served under the same commander year after year. This produced a strong sense of team spirit or cohesion within the English armies from around 1360 onwards that other European armies simply failed to match. Foreign chroniclers recorded again and again that English armies were basically just that - English. They were not the feudal levies raised by great lords from their peasants. This was to have a profound impact on English society as noblemen and knights came to see themselves as national team leaders with close links to the men who served them, be it in arms or as tenant farmers. In return the soldiers and peasants viewed the nobles as their local leaders and champions, turning to the local noble when in difficulty or needing help of some kind. On the continent, by contrast, nobles came to see themselves as part of a social caste that had closer links to the nobles of other countries than to the peasants of their own. The peasants reciprocated by viewing the nobles as remote and unhelpful figures. The social trends were slow to develop, but were all the stronger for that. In later centuries the differences would help explain why Europe erupted into revolutions, while Britain did not.

While some indentures were between knights and nobles, the majority were with the king directly. Even those that were between subjects were for moneys that originated with the king, and could be withheld by him. As with the militia system it was a system that was designed to provide the king with a near monopoly of armed might. However, the individual commanders did enjoy a degree of freedom. They could choose not to serve one year, for example, if the deal on offer was not to their liking.

In the context of the Wars of the Roses, the fact that the provision of armed men was in the hands of nobles and knights has been used by some historians to suggest that armies could be raised quickly for anyone who could pay. Things

The Battle of Losecoat Field 1470

were not that simple, however. By the 1450s English soldiers were habitually loyal to the crown. A commander who sought to recruit his usual men to fight against the king might, and sometimes did, find himself unable to recruit anyone.

Again it was York's claim to be raising men to rescue King Henry VI from his evil advisers that proved crucial. Nearly everyone knew that the administration of the kingdom was in a dire state and so could accept that serving the Yorkist cause was not rebellion, but true loyalty. Not everyone agreed, of course, and many remained loyal to Henry even though they despised Margaret and her cronies.

The most numerous mercenaries in English armies serving in France had been Welsh. At this date Wales had ceased to be an independent country, or rather a collection of them, but had not yet been fully integrated into the English systems of government. The Welsh did not, therefore, provide militias or indentured retinues. Instead they provided companies of men recruited by royal officials.

This hobilar, or pricker, is typical of Wars of the Roses cavalry. He wears a helmet of metal padded with wool. His leather sleeveless jack has overlapping metal plates and is worn over a mail shirt that reaches to the elbows and to mid-thigh. His leg armour is made of plate and covers him from upper thigh to toe. For weapons he has a long but light lance, backed by a sword. Such men had many uses on campaign, but few on the battlefield.

The Battle of Losecoat Field 1470

A typical Welsh company consisted of 100 men, four cooks, one translator (few Welshmen spoke English), one standard bearer, one crier (a man with a loud voice to shout out commands) one physician and a commander. Most of the men were archers, but about a quarter were men armed with spears or poleaxes whose task was to protect the archers from cavalry or other attack.

Irishmen were also hired as mercenaries. They tended to be lightly armed men mounted on small ponies. Few of these Irish horsemen were armoured, other than a helmet, with only the leaders having mail coats or plate breastplates. For weaponry the Irish carried two or three light javelins, plus a sword or long knife.

On campaign in France, the Irish horsemen were used to scout ahead and to the flanks of the army. They could fight skirmishes with small numbers of French, capture peasants for questioning and forage for food, but were not much use in battle against the French.

The Scots and French were never hired as mercenaries as they were regarded as the national enemies of England, but other foreigners were hired in numbers. Most of these men came from Germany or the Low Countries. They had contracts not too dissimilar to the indentures that recruited English soldiers. The men were recruited by a local knight or lord, who then agreed a deal with his employer. While the English had scruples about fighting their monarch, the foreign mercenaries had no such issues. They would cheerfully fight for whoever paid them.

The majority of mercenaries serving in the Wars of the Roses were specialists. Typical were the handgunners and petardiers. Handgunners were equipped with guns that consisted of a tube of iron, open at one end. The gunpowder and lead pellet were pushed down from the open end with a rammer. A hot iron wire or burning coal was then thrust into a small hole at the closed end which set off the charge and propelled the lead pellet out the other end. These early hand guns produced a huge amount of smoke and noise, which could serve to frighten horses and unsettle inexperienced troops, but their actual effectiveness as weapons is unclear. They seem to have had a range not much short of the longbow, but their rate of fire was much slower - about one shot every minute or so compared to a longbow shooting ten arrows a minute. At close range they were more effective for the heavy lead pellet could pass straight through one man to kill or wound the man behind, something an arrow could not do.

Petardiers were equipped with petards, clay pots about five inches across that were filled with gunpowder and scraps of old iron or pottery. A fuse entered the

The Battle of Losecoat Field 1470

petard and was lit before the pot was thrown at the enemy. The range of a petard was obviously limited, but again at close quarters they could be horrific weapons. A petard exploding among a densely packed formation of infantry could kill or wound many men, opening up a gap in the formation that could prove fatal if it were quickly exploited.

Because these men had no scruples, all the senior noblemen engaged in the Wars of the Roses hired them in numbers. In 1461 the Earl of Warwick hired 500 handgunners from Burgundy for the summer and in 1485 Henry Tudor had over a thousand.

Artillery were also to be seen on battlefields during the Wars of the Roses, manned by either foreign mercenaries or English gunners. The really big cannon, bombards able to hurl stones weighing 200lb, were not seen on battlefields. They were massively expensive to make, difficult to transport and virtually immobile on the battlefield. Essential in sieges, they were simply too big and heavy for battles. Battlefield artillery went by a variety of names, though culverine and serpentine seem to have been popular. These guns had barrels about eight to 12 feet long and fired stone or iron shot weighing about 10 to 20lb. The cannon were mounted on carriages that had two large wheels and a long wooden trail behind. The trail was used to pull the gun around the battlefield, or swivel it from side to side before firing. The barrel could be raised or lowered with a wooden

This handgunner is based on an English manuscript dating to about 1470. His gun is an iron tube closed at one end. Gunpowder and bullet were rammed down the open end and fired by inserting a hot wire into a hole at the closed end. He wears a mail shirt reaching almost to elbows and knees. Over this is a short-sleeved shirt of padded wool. His open faced helmet is of iron, probably padded with wool. His knees are protected by iron plates, but his legs and lower arms are otherwise unprotected. He has a sword for use at close quarters once he has fired his gun.

wedge to alter the range. On the move the trail was fixed to a cart containing the ammunition and pulled by oxen or horses. There was usually at least one other cart filled with ammunition.

What all these guns and firearms had in common was their complete unpredictability. Even in the hands of a trained and experienced gunner, the weapons would behave completely differently one day to how they did the next. The problem was the gunpowder.

At this date making gunpowder was more of an art that a science. Nobody understood the chemical reactions involved, so getting the mix right was down to trial and error, with each gunner fiercely guarding his own preferred method. Of the three ingredients, charcoal was by far the cheapest and easiest to source. Sulphur was more expensive, but again not too difficult to come by. It was saltpetre that really represented the problem.

Saltpetre, as its name meaning "salt-rock" suggests could be mined, but only in a very few places. Most countries resorted to manufacturing saltpetre. This was a messy and protracted business that involved collecting together large quantities of horse, cattle or sheep manure, mixing it with wood ash and piling it up inside a wooden barn which had a waterproof floor of rammed clay. The organic mass was then wetted thoroughly each week with human urine for a year. Then the wetting was stopped and the barn sealed shut to allow the rotting mass to dry out gradually. As the water evaporated slowly from the surface of the putrid mess, it brought to the surface raw saltpetre which precipitated out as white crystals. Each cubic yard of manure produced about 16lb of saltpetre.

The saltpetre produced by this method was a mix of various organic nitrates, the composition of which varied with the quality of the raw materials, the temperatures at which it rotted and the time allowed for drying. Each batch of saltpetre had its own qualities that affected the performance of the gunpowder that it was used to make. Very often the crucial feature of this crude saltpetre proved to be its hydrostatic properties. All saltpetre will absorb water from the air if left uncovered, but certain forms of raw saltpetre will absorb it more quickly than others. On damp days the saltpetre will suck up moisture faster than ever. And damp saltpetre meant gunpowder that did not explode very well.

Gunpowder in the 15th century was a simple mix of charcoal, sulphur and saltpetre for as yet no way had been found of combining the three into a stable powder. Each of these three has a quite different density, so if a barrel of mixed gunpowder was put onto a cart and trundled over the bumpy roads of the period

The Battle of Losecoat Field 1470

for any amount of time the three components would separate out. Before a barrel of gunpowder could be used it had to be tumbled around the ground for quite some time to remix the ingredients. It was more usual, therefore, for the ingredients to be transported separately and for the gunpowder to be mixed only when it was needed.

The gunpowder then had to "proved" before it could be used. This generally involved putting a measured quantity of powder into a handgun and ramming down a lead pellet of known weight. The gun was then fired, with the gunner watching carefully to gauge the force and sound of the explosion, as well as the distance the shot was carried. From this the gunner could then work out how much powder should be used to produce a standard explosive force. The powder would then be parceled up into separate cloth bags accordingly.

As can be imagined, getting guns ready to fire was a laborious, lengthy and highly skilled business. Even then things did not always go right. As recently as 1460 King James II of Scotland was to be killed when a cannon burst as he fired it.

For centuries the battlefield had been ruled by the armoured knight on horseback. A well timed charge by heavy horsemen had been able to smash enemy formations and win a battle with ease. From 1346 onwards, however, the English

Most armoured infantry during the Wars of the Roses were armed something like this figure. He wears an iron helmet and full upper harness composed of breastplate with groin plates over a mail shirt. His lower arms and hands are protected by plate armour gauntlets. His legs are quite unprotected. His main weapon is a bill, a weapon on a shaft over six feet long that combined a thrusting point with a chopping blade and sometimes, as here, a back hook to pull enemies to the ground. The bill was based on a farmer's hedging tool and was a distinctively English weapon. He has a sword to use in case his bill breaks or for close infighting.

The Battle of Losecoat Field 1470

had rendered this tactic obsolete with a novel tactical formation. The English put their armoured men on foot, drawn up in a line between four and eight ranks deep. The men stood shoulder to shoulder to form a solid block of men. A high proportion of these men were armed with pole weapons of one sort or another. At first these were mostly spears, but by the time of the Wars of the Roses these had mostly been replaced by bills. Horses will not run headlong into a solid barrier, be it a brick wall or a mass of men. So long as the men on foot stood their ground, charging cavalry would come to a halt. The horsemen would then be vulnerable to the pole weapons of the infantry.

Standing on the flanks of the densely packed armoured infantry were bodies of archers. What made archery so effective was the fact that the archers were using a tactic that became known as the arrowstorm. Instead of the archers being dispersed among the arrayed infantry they were grouped together as solid groups of archers. This enabled them for the first time to come under the command of an experienced knight whose sole task was to direct the archery. A group of archers could be ordered to shoot at the same time at the same target.

What made the arrowstorm effective was a realisation that the archers did not

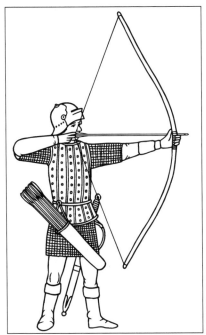

This archer is typical of the period. Because large numbers of archers served on both sides he is wearing fairly substantial armour to provide protection against incoming arrows. He has a mail shirt reaching to elbows and knees. Over this he wears a sleeveless jack made of up to 22 layers of linen over which are stitched plates of iron or horn. His sallet-style helmet is of steel, padded with wool. His lower arms are free to allow him to draw his bow. The lower legs are unarmoured, probably to allow him to move nimbly around the battlefield. His bow is the standard longbow of the period and he has a quiver of arrows at his belt. His sword and buckler are for hand to hand fighting.

actually need to aim to hit a particular man, nor even a group of men. Such a feat was beyond most archers at ranges over 100 yards. Instead all the archers needed to do was to shoot in the given direction at a given range. Even the most average archer could put an arrow to within 20 yards or so of a chosen spot at 200 yards range.

A single archer making such a shot would have little impact, but by grouping the archers together in numbers and making them all shoot at once the situation was transformed. A force of 200 archers would put 200 arrows simultaneously down into a designated area. The scattering of arrows by mediocre aiming would matter little, and indeed would help ensure that the arrows hit something.

The lack of a need for precision aiming speeded up the business of shooting. Instead of it taking up to 20 seconds to knock an arrow, choose a target, draw and shoot, archers could now knock, point in the right direction and let fly in just 10 seconds. If arrows were put point downward in the turf in front of the archer instead of being kept in the quiver, the shooting time per arrow was down to 6 seconds. It became usual for each archer to put about six arrows in front of him preparatory to shooting.

The combined results of these changes was awesome. The archery commander would watch the developing battle and select an enemy formation to be the target for his men. When the enemy came within range, the commander would point out the direction and call a range. The archers would then begin shooting, each man letting fly six arrows in 24 seconds or so.

At the receiving end the result was a veritable storm of arrows. Contemporary writers, awed by the sight, compared the arrows to falling hail or rain. A force of 500 archers could put 2400 arrows into an area of battlefield measuring 40 metres square with ease. Such a concentration of missiles in such a small space would guarantee that any man or horse in that patch of ground would be almost guaranteed to be hit by at least one arrow. No wonder contemporaries were so awed.

There would then follow a short pause while the archers got more arrows from their quivers and pushed them into the ground in front of them. The commander would use this time to assess the damage inflicted on the enemy, scan the battlefield for the next most urgent target and decide whom to shoot at next. Again the commander would point and call out a range, again the arrowstorm would be let fly. Of course, such tactics were enormously costly in terms of arrows, and arrows were not cheap. Only kings or the richest nobles could afford to supply

The Battle of Losecoat Field 1470

large numbers of archers. It was reckoned that each archer needed 400 arrows for a campaign, and with each arrow costing a penny that was expensive.

By the Wars of the Roses the arrowstorm had become slightly less decisive. Knights usually fought on foot and new types of armour had been invented. This new armour took the form of steel plates shaped to wrap around the body. The plate armour was also designed to have smooth shapes and flowing profiles so that an arrow would glance off it more easily. Even so the new armour was not entirely proof against arrows. Given the huge numbers of arrows shot during battles at this period some at least would find a weak spot and penetrate to the man's flesh. Even if that did not happen the sheer force of an arrow strike was considerable. An arrow had more than enough momentum to knock a man over, or to daze him badly if it hit his helmet. Moreover many men could not afford such very expensive armour and so went into battle only partially armoured, or wearing old fashioned mail that was less proof against arrows.

Nevertheless the usual battlefield tactic at this date was still to deploy knights and men at arms in a solid phalanx, flanked by archers. Sometimes groups of archers were put at intervals along the line of armoured men. While the archers were effective at a distance, they were vulnerable to armoured infantry at close quarters and so they might fall back behind the men at arms when the enemy closed to hand to hand fighting. More heavily armoured archers, as was increasingly common by the later 15th century, would join the hand to hand fighting.

Many commanders sought to put their infantry into defensive positions of one sort or another. These might be behind field boundary hedges or ditches, inside villages or even specially dug fieldworks.

A new factor by the time of the Wars of the Roses was the advent of guns. These came in two forms: handguns and artillery. For the most part these made relatively little impact on tactical dispositions on the battlefield. Hand guns increased the death rate in the last few yards before the men got to work with hand weapons, while artillery increased the number of deaths at a distance. However, neither were so deadly as to alter the dispositions or tactical formations. The bigger guns rendered useless the old stone walled castles, one reason why sieges were relatively rare in the Wars of the Roses.

Although heavily armoured, mounted knights had fallen out of use there was still a role for horsemen. As noted above, Irish horsemen were sometimes hired to serve as scouts, but most commanders preferred to use Englishmen equipped

The Battle of Losecoat Field 1470

A standard infantry formation from the Wars of the Roses. The armoured billmen and men at arms are formed up four ranks deep in the centre while the archers are pushed forward on the flanks to shoot at the advancing enemy. The commanding knight and his assistants stand behind to direct movement.

as hobilars. These hobilars - also known as currours or prickers - were more lightly armed than knights and rode less expensive horses. Their roles were mostly off the battlefield. They scouted ahead and to the flanks of the army looking for the enemy. They rode ahead to secure bridges or fords. They rode off to carry messages to other commanders or to local authorities. They sought good campsites, bought - or in France stole - food supplies.

Even on the field of battle these hobilars had a use. They were kept in reserve to be unleashed on a fleeing enemy to use their speed to ride down fugitives. Or they could be thrown into action to disrupt a pursuit by enemy horsemen and so cover the retreat of the infantry. There were some occasions, admittedly rare, when hobilars performed a mounted charge. This tactic was rarely used as it was so rarely successful. Against formed infantry it was doomed to failure, but if they could catch infantry on the march or out of formation after crossing a stream then the hobilars could perform great service.

During the Wars of the Roses it was customary for an army to be divided into three "battles". Each battle consisted of a mix of soldier types, with archers and men at arms. The commander of the army usually took command of the central battle, with his more experienced subordinate leading the foreward battle and the third commander the rear battle. Any artillery present was usually kept with the central battle, as much for its commercial value as its use in fighting. Hobilars or other mounted troops would usually be formed outside this traditional structure. They would have their own commander answerable to the army commander, but would only rarely be actually with the army itself. More often the bulk of these men were off on detached duties of one kind or another, though rarely more than a day or two's ride from the army.

It was traditional for the central battle to be the largest, perhaps as strong as the other two put together. Some commanders preferred to vary this arrangement. The most usual variation was to increase the strength of the advance battle to make it capable of independent action. Some army commanders even preferred to put themselves in charge of the advance battle, delegating the central battle to the third in command.

It had become customary for English armies to be under the command of a nobleman - often the king or a prince of royal blood when campaigning in France. This was largely for political and social reasons. Nobles who had brought sizeable forces to the war could be relied upon to take orders from a social superior. However, senior nobles with great military talent were in short supply, so the English kings had got into the habit of appointing one or more highly experienced and skilful soldiers to be Constables to give advice to the nobleman in command. The exact nature of the relationship between the Constables and the noble commander is not known. Presumably there were times when the nobleman was only nominally in charge, with everyone present knowing that the Constable was the real man in charge. At other times a nobleman of talent would use his Constable more in the role of chief of staff to look after the more mundane organisational tasks of an army on the move.

In the context of the Wars of the Roses, armies tended to be commanded by

The Battle of Losecoat Field 1470

the most politically important nobleman present. It tended to be these men who had called the army into existence and who decided what its purpose was to be. There were usually Constables present, and here their role seems to have been to offer advice when asked for it. They might be asked their opinion on any matter, but it was always up the nobleman in charge what decision to make. It was, in a very real sense, his head that was going to be on the block if anything went wrong.

The deployment of handgunners is not fully understood. One possible explanation has them forming much of the front rank of an infantry formation surrounded by armoured infantry. The knightly commander of the unit stands behind to shout orders.

Chapter 4
The Battle of Losecoat Field

Sometime in 1469 two landholders in Lincolnshire fell out over a piece of land. The dispute grew bitter as both sides refused any offer of mediation and began seeking friends and supporters among their neighbours. Whatever the rights and wrongs of the original dispute, the spreading storm had important connotations.

Sir Thomas Burgh of Gainsborough was one party to the argument. He came from an ancient and wealthy Lincolnshire family, though one that had never risen to the nobility. He himself had served as MP for Gainsborough and Sheriff of Lincolnshire. Although the Burgh family was not openly loyal to either side during the earlier bout of fighting, Sir Thomas did find favour with Edward IV it the early 1460s. When Edward rode away from the Earl of Warwick's Middleham Castle in 1469, he made straight for Gainsborough to seek support and protection from Burgh. Sir Thomas had called out his retainers and escorted the king south while both wondered if Warwick would launch a treacherous attack. Edward therefore owed Burgh a personal favour.

The other man involved in the dispute was Richard, Lord Welles. Socially and materially, Welles was a cut above Burgh. His estates were wide and wealthy, while he himself came from a family that had been ennobled seven generations earlier. He was well connected and popular. In 1461 he had been on the Lancastrian side at the First Battle of St Albans, but he had soon convinced the Yorkists that he had acted out of loyalty to King Henry. By 1463 he was pardoned and returned to his estates. Not only was Welles a wealthy baron, he had attracted to his cause his two brothers in law, Sir Thomas of Lande and Sir Thomas Dymmock. Both these men were wealthy, and Dymmock was the Royal Champion of England. This was a largely ceremonial role, but it did involve the holder in close contact with the monarch - so Edward was again involved.

The Battle of Losecoat Field 1470

At Christmas, Welles took advantage of his rival's absence to attack Burgh's newly completed grand house of Gainsborough Hall. Welles's men looted the house thoroughly, roughed up the servants who tried to stop them and then set fire to the magnificent house as they were leaving. The flames failed to catch hold and what is now Gainsborough Old Hall stands to this day. It is open to the public and may be hired for weddings.

When Edward heard of the attack on Gainsborough Hall, he was furious. The last thing he needed at this awkward moment was nobles resorting to violence to sort out private disputes. He summoned Welles, Dymmock and Burgh to come to London. They arrived early in February and Edward listened testily while they explained themselves. Edward dismissed them, saying he would himself stop off in Lincolnshire during a planned journey north to look into the matter and reach a decision. Something about Edward's behaviour alarmed Lord Welles. That night he fled in darkness to Westminster Abbey where he hurried to the high altar and cried out that was seeking sanctuary. Next day, Edward sent a message telling Welles his life was not in jeapardy and even granting all three Lincolnshire men a pardon for their actions.

That same day word came from Lincoln that riots and demonstrations had broken out. At first details were sparse, but the trouble did not seem to be directly related to the Burgh-Dymmock-Welles dispute. The previous year a mysterious man calling himself Robin of Redesdale had stirred up trouble in Lincolnshire in support of Warwick. The local nobles had soon put down the disturbances, and killed Robin of Redesdale, and Edward had issued a general pardon to all those involved on condition that they swore an oath of personal loyalty to him. The current unrest was being caused by a new man calling himself Robin of Redesdale. He was riding round the county saying that Edward was coming north with an army to execute all the men who had been involved in the previous uprising. Mass executions and confiscations of property were planned, said Robin of Redesdale. The fact that three notable landowners had been summoned to London by Edward lent credence to the rumours.

Edward reacted on 3 March by summoning the royal artillery to be ready to leave London next day, and calling out the militia of 12 counties to meet him at mustering points on the Great North Road over the following week as he headed north from London to Lincoln. For the campaign that

The Battle of Losecoat Field 1470

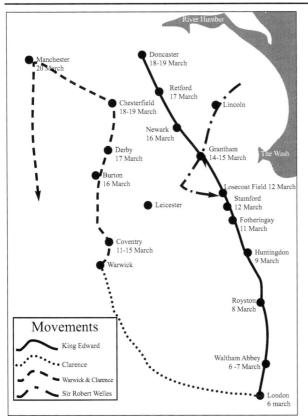

The movement of the main protagonists in the Battle of Losecoat Field. It was the mustering of a rebellious demonstration just outside Lincoln that caused the campaign, though it did not really get under way until Edward IV left London on 6 March

followed we are fortunate in having an account written by an unknown official of the Royal household. The man did not put his name to the account, but he was clearly a fairly senior official as he was privy to the king's letters and the military payments made. Of course, this account sees things very much from Edward's point of view and since no version of events from the other side has survived we may have a rather biased record of what happened.

Although he had intended to march out of London on 4 March, Edward delayed when he received a note from his brother Clarence. Clarence said that he was on his way to visit his wife in the West Country, but was diverting by way of London as he had news from Lincolnshire. Clarence arrived on 6 March. The brothers attended a church service at St Paul's

Cathedral, then went to their mother's house for a meal and talks. Clarence said that the reports from Lincoln were overblown and that there had merely been some demonstrations and protests about Edward's supposed revenge. Edward responded that he had no intention of taking revenge but was going to Lincolnshire only to investigate the land dispute, but now that there was rioting he was taking an army with him.

Edward marched out of London that afternoon along with the royal artillery, the Earl of Arundel, Lord Hastings and Sir Henry Percy. As soon as he was gone, Clarence dashed off to speak to Lord Welles for an hour or so. He then rode out of London, but instead of heading southwest to his wife he rode northwest for an unknown destination. A messenger with news of Clarence's action left at once and caught up with Edward that night at Waltham Abbey.

Next morning, Edward sent gallopers with messages for several men. He ordered Clarence to come to meet him in Grantham, and sent a message to Warwick with an identical request. Edward ordered the officials in Lincoln to send him an up to date report on conditions in the county.

That rider going north passed a messenger hurrying south with news from Gainsborough. That message brought alarming news. Sir Robert Welles, eldest son of Lord Welles, was now calling himself Great Captain of the Commons of Lincolnshire. Not only that but he had sent men to every church in Lincolnshire the previous Sunday, 4 March, to read out a proclamation. This had repeated the accusation that Edward was coming to destroy the people of Lincolnshire, then added that all those who loved justice and Lincolnshire should come fully armed to Ranby Hawe on 6 March to show Edward that the county would not take things lying down. Welles had also summoned his retainers and was offering to pay other soldiers to join his cause. Edward sent another man riding south ordering Welles, Dymmock and Burgh to come to join him on the road north, no doubt intending to question them over the behaviour of Sir Robert Welles.

Edward reached Royston that night to find a message from Clarence there. This stated that Clarence had heard of the new trouble and was riding to join Warwick before heading for Grantham. Edward sent a letter of thanks back, giving Clarence authority to raise the militia of Warwickshire and Worcedstershire and bring them to Grantham. As Edward set out from Royston on the morning of 9 March he got a message from the Steward of

The Battle of Losecoat Field 1470

Gainsborough Old Hall as it stands today. It was an apparently trivial provincial feud involving this country house, then new, which sparked the trail of events that was to lead to bloodshed on the fields of Rutland.

Tattershall Castle. This stated that the men of Lincolnshire were turning out in large numbers to join Sir Robert Welles and that large reinforcements were expected from Yorkshire. The letter ended with the alarming estimate that Welles would by the end of the week have 100,000 men with him.

Undeterred, Edward marched on to Huntingdon, arriving on the evening of 9 March. Late that night Welles and Dymmock arrived under armed

The Battle of Losecoat Field 1470

escort - Burgh was apparently not with them. On the morning of 10 March Edward questioned them closely. According to the source in Edward's entourage Welles acknowledged that before he had left for London he and his son had agreed to foment further trouble, spreading the rumour that Edward would come to execute the men of Lincolnshire. Welles also said that Dymmock had been in on the plan, thinking it would put added pressure on Edward to decide the land dispute in their favour.

Edward's response is not recorded, but it was enough to persuade Lord Welles to write a letter to his son. Sir Robert was reported still to have been in Lincoln on the morning of 9 March, but to have been preparing to move very soon. The letter written by Lord Welles instructed Sir Robert Welles to disband his army immediately, to come to Grantham to submit to Edward and to leave the arms of his men piled in Lincoln. Ominously the letter stated that Edward had promised to hold Lord Welles responsible for his son's actions.

That had all taken some time, so Edward and his gathering army did not leave Huntingdon until late in the day. They evening they got as far as Fotheringhay Castle, an old property of Edward's family. He and his nobles stayed in the castle while the army camped in the fields outside. A message came in from Lincoln saying that Sir Robert Welles and his force had left on the morning of the 10th. The rebel army was estimated to be about 30,000 strong. The word had been that the army was marching to Grantham to block Edward's route to Lincolnshire. However, the message said that an informer in Welles's inner circle had reported that in fact the force was heading to Leicester to meet reinforcements. This was puzzling to Edward, as Leicester was an odd rendezvous for the reinforcements expected from Yorkshire.

At dawn next morning, Monday 12 March, Edward marched out of Fotheringhay. He had not gone far towards Stamford when a messenger arrived from Clarence. This letter had been written on the morning of the 11 March at Coventry. The message said that Clarence was now with the Earl of Warwick, who had mustered a fine army to come to help Edward. They were about to leave for Grantham and expected to arrive sometime on Tuesday 13 March having come by way of Leicester. Leicester again. Edward sat down at a table and himself wrote out a letter of thanks to Clarence and Warwick.

The Battle of Losecoat Field 1470

Early on Monday 12 March Edward reached Stamford. He was unwilling to move further north until he had definite news of the enemy. A rider came from Grantham to report that Welles and his men had left that town the previous day, heading southwest towards Leicester.

Edward sent out his mounted hobilars to scout the road from Grantham to Leicester by way of Melton Mowbray. It was expected to be some hours

In 1470 Fotheringhay Castle was as stout and easily defended a castle as any in England. It was here that Edward IV spent the night before the battle. The castle was demolished in the 1640s after it had fallen into disrepair. All that remains visible today is this large earthen mound on the banks of the River Nene just east of the village of Fotheringhay, Northamptonshire.

before the scouts reached that main road, now the A607, and got back again. Edward told his men they could rest, eat and relax.

In fact it was barely an hour before the first scouts came galloping into Stamford. Sir Robert Welles and his men were not heading to Leicester at all. They were barely five miles away at Empingham, advancing down the road toward Stamford with banners unfurled and armed for battle. At this date the unfurling of banners signified that combat was expected shortly. Clearly the rebels were intending to attack the royal army.

Edward hurriedly roused his men, getting them armed for action and set off toward Empingham. Edward's scouts were keeping close eyes on the rebels. As soon as they had realised that they had been discovered the rebels had turned east, heading for the high ground north of Tickencote astride the main road north. This is now the A1, a busy dual carriageway, but in 1470 was the Great North Road. It was already old then, having been built by the Romans in around ad67. Edward accordingly changed his route of march, going up the Great North Road.

Just north of the village of Great Casterton Edward and his army crested a rise. Here they found the royal hobilars waiting for them and keeping a watch on the rebels. Sir Robert Welles had his men deployed astride the Great North Road on the crest of a ridge now marked by the farm of Tickencote Warren. The messages that Edward had been receiving from his supporters about the rebel army gave various estimates for its size. Some of these were vague - saying only that it was "large".

The steward of Tattershall had estimated that it was very big and would soon number 100,000. However he had not seen the army itself and was merely reporting rumour. The royal agent in Lincoln had given a more definite figure of 30,000 men. He had seen the gathering host with his own eyes and might have known what he was talking about. But estimating numbers of men in a crowd is a notoriously difficult business, even today giving an accurate figure for people on a demonstration march is near to impossible with police and organisers giving very different figures. Most people tend to overestimate, so maybe the anonymous Yorkist in Lincoln did likewise.

Modern historians tend to discount medieval estimates of army sizes almost completely. One modern historian has hazarded a guesss that the rebels may have had 10,000 men present, but in fact nobody can be certain.

The Battle of Losecoat Field 1470

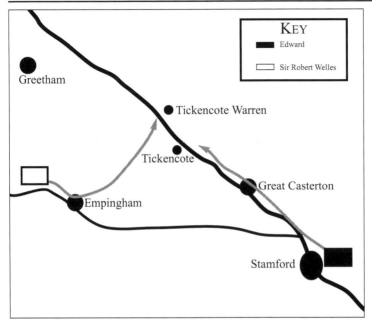

The approach to the battle on the morning of 12 March 1470. Sir Robert Welles and the rebels were advancing on Edward IV's camp at Stamford when Edward's scouts sighted them at Empingham. Welles then turned aside to seek a defensive position.

We can be a little more certain about the composition of the army than about its size. The anonymous man with Edward's army says that nearly the entire rebel force was on foot. This would make sense. The rumours that Welles had been spreading concerned the supposed revenge that Edward was going to take on the common men of Lincolnshire for their involvement in the rioting under Robin of Redesdale the previous year. This would indicate that few of the gentry and none of the nobility were expected to join the rising. War horses were expensive things and few ordinary men could afford them.

The fighting quality of the rebels is something of a debating point. As discussed in an earlier chapter the militia tended to have good quality armour and weaponry, and to have undergone military training of a reasonably high standard. These militia men could be expected to fight well and skillfully. On the other hand the militia had not been called out. Sir Robert Welles had been using the title Great Captain of the Commons of Lincolnshire, but he had made no attempt to adopt or usurp any official titles. He had made a direct appeal to the men of Lincolnshire through the speeches read out at churches on 4 March. It may be that some, perhaps

The Battle of Losecoat Field 1470

many, militia men responded to the call. But however many did march, they went as individual men not as formed units under their commanders. That inevitably weakened their effectiveness.

The other infantry in the rebel force will have been farm workers or townsmen who had picked up whatever weaponry came to hand. Such men were not often seen in battles during the Wars of the Roses. The increasing sophistication of weaponry and of armour was making waging war an expensive and specialised business. The days when a man could pick up a spear and shield for the cost of a few days pay and be as well equipped as most men in an army were long gone. Without modern armour and weapons a man, no matter how strong or brave, would be of little use on a battlefield by the later 15th century. This fact was not fully appreciated among men who had not been to war. Untrained, poorly equipped men would often join demonstrations and rioting, but no sensible commander took such men into a pitched battle. That Sir Robert Welles had sizeable numbers of such men with him says much about his inexperience, and shows that he probably did not expect to get involved in serious fighting.

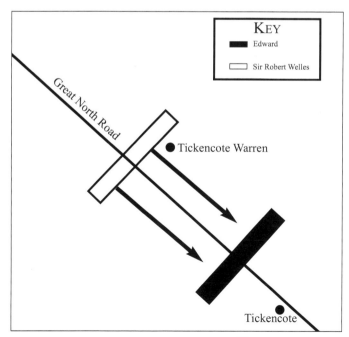

Welles drew up his men on a ridge looking down a long gentle slope to Tickencote. Edward arrayed his army on flat ground before opening fire with his artillery. The artillery fire induced Welles to launch a rash attack down the slope at Edward's veterans.

The Battle of Losecoat Field 1470

Welles drew his men up in a single formation astride the Great North Road. It would have made sense for the better armoured men to be in the front ranks, but whether or not Welles did this we do not know. We do know that Welles walked out in front of his army as Edward's force began to come within sight. Presumably he was dressing the ranks and making short speeches of encouragement - the usual tasks of a medieval commander as battle approached.

It was probably just north of Tickencote Laund that Edward arrayed his army for battle. This was just over half a mile south of Welles's position and on a fairly large area of flat land halfway up the long slope that led from Great Casterton to the ridge where Welles was. He would have been

A peaceful view across the battlefield today.

The Battle of Losecoat Field 1470

out of bowshot range, but within sight. And he wanted Sir Robert Welles to see what was going to happen next.

At the time nobody recorded how big Edward's army was on the day of the Battle of Losecoat Field. It is known that Edward had fewer men than did Sir Robert Welles, but since we cannot be certain how many men Welles had that does not help much.

We know that a large part of his cavalry were off looking for the rebels near Melton Mowbray, but even so Edward had considerably more horsemen than did the rebels. Most of these men will have been hobilars, but there would probably have been a small number of more heavily armoured men.

Edward's infantry at this battle would have comprised his own personal retainers, plus those of Arundel, Hastings and the other noblemen present. These retainers were professional soldiers and while we don't know how many of them were present they would have been considered the heart of the royal army. Edward also had a fair number of militia men with him. He had called out several county militia and ordered them to meet him on the road north from London. Ordinarily these commissions of array would have raised as many as 15,000 men, but given the speed with which Edward was marching it is unlikely that more than a fraction of this number appeared in time. Certainly some units were still marching north up the Great North Road hoping to catch up with Edward while the battle was taking place.

Where Edward undoubtedly had an advantage was in artillery. He had the royal artillery train, the rebels had no cannon at all. This may not have been as great an advantage as it might appear to modern readers since late 15th century artillery was unreliable, inaccurate and of shorter range than is often realised. Nevertheless these guns could fire cannonballs at least as far as a longbow could shoot while the noise, fire and smoke they produced were very impressive to men unaccustomed to them. Nor should the effect on morale of an incoming cannonball be dismissed. A sword could slice a man's head off, an arrow could pierce him from front to back, but only a cannonball could reduce him in an instant to such a mess of bloody pulp that it was impossible to see where his head, torso or arms had been. Seeing one's comrades destroyed in such grisly fashion was a massive blow to medieval morale.

The Battle of Losecoat Field 1470

But before battle could be joined, Edward had a task to perform. Lord Welles and Sir Thomas Dymmock were brought forward to stand in front of his army, facing toward the rebel force. Sir Robert Welles and Sir Richard Warren could be seen watching. Edward reminded Welles and Dymmock that in London in February he had generously granted them pardons for their actions over the winter. But that they had repaid him by helping to organise the uprising that now saw the men of Lincolnshire arrayed for battle on the ridge of Tickencote. He declared that he had told Sir Robert Welles that his father would be held responsible if the uprising did not disband at once. It had not disbanded, and so Lord Welles was as guilty of treason as was his son.

Thereupon Edward ordered that the heads of Wells and Dymmock be sliced off. A burly retainer stepped forward and did the deed. The severed heads of the two men were picked up by their hair and displayed first to Edward's army and then to the rebels.

Either at this point, or perhaps slightly earlier as the contemporary accounts are unclear, Sir Robert Welles put off his own surcoat. The surcoat was a thin robe of linen or wool that was worn over armour. It was

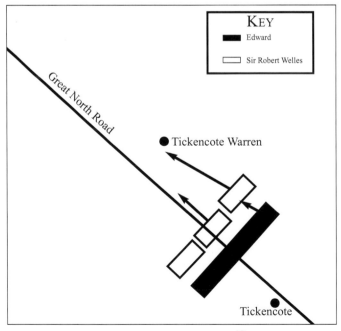

The disintegration of the rebel army probably started on their left wing, which seems to have suffered most from the royal artillery in the early stages of the battle.

The Battle of Losecoat Field 1470

decorated with the arms or badge of the wearer or the nobleman he supported. Edward, for instance, had the badge of a sun in splendour. Welles then put on a new surcoat, this one prominently displaying a black bull. The black bull was the badge of the Duke of Clarence. Other men in Welles's army put on identical surcoats, others donned surcoats showing a bear chained to a ragged staff - the badge of the Earl of Warwick.

The anonymous writer in Edward's staff continues "and so forthwith proceding against these said rebels, by the help of Almighty God, he achieved the victory, and distressed more than 30,000 men, using therewith plentiously of his mercy in the saving of the lives of his poor and wretched commons." This rather terse and short account by an undoubted eyewitness has induced many modern historians to think that the battle was short and over quickly. They envisage Edward leading a charge against the rebels that defeated them and put them to rout. However, the writer was more interested in the politics and effects of the campaign than in the fighting itself, so it is possible that he was not really interested in the progress of the battle itself.

Another chronicler, John Warkworth, Master of Peterhouse College, Cambridge, gives a different account of the battle. Warkworth was not at the battle, but he spoke to several men who had been. According to Warkworth, the executions of Welles and Dymmock were followed by a pause, after which Edward's cannon opened fire. Edward had had his men drag these guns all the way from London, so it would be only natural for him to want to use the things - especially as the day was dry and so the cannon could be used reliably. But there was more to the move than that.

The cannon of the time outranged longbows. This meant that the royal artillery could shoot at the rebels, while the rebels could not respond at all. The artillery may have been slow in firing compared to later guns, and to contemporary bows, but they would have had an horrific effect on the densely packed ranks of the rebels. Each incoming shot would have ploughed through the ranks, killing or disabling several men as it tore its way through flesh and bone. It would not have been long before Welles ordered the advance. If he stayed where he was his men would have been killed. And since they had the advantage of the slope in their favour, the rebels could charge down on the royal army with greater momentum.

But this was exactly what Edward wanted. As the poorly trained and ill-

The Battle of Losecoat Field 1470

equipped rebels came down the slope they chanted two distinct battle cries "Clarence" and "A Warwick". Combined with their choice of surcoats the rebels were clearly claiming to be acting on behalf of the Earl of Warwick and Duke of Clarence. Whether they were or not was not clear to Edward at the time. Probably his mind was elsewhere as he had a battle to fight and win.

Artillery in the 1470s could fire only slowly. Most likely as the rebels advanced the royal artillery had time to fire only once or twice. Of greater impact would have been the longbows of the retainers and militia. As the rebels got even closer handguns would have been fired to punch holes through armour and helmets to kill the men wearing them. Suddenly the left wing of the rebels turned and fled. The panic spread along the rebel line, with the centre turning next and finally the right wing.

The men of Lincolnshire cannot be blamed for turning tail and running. They were not professional soldiers and had not come to fight a pitched battle. As with many medieval risings they were more intent on a riotous demonstration than on a war. Moreover they had been misled by Sir Robert

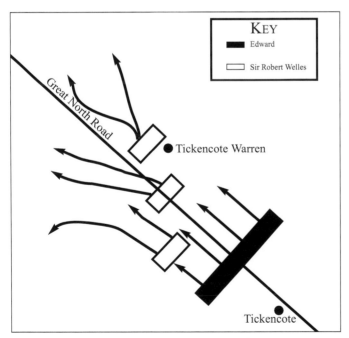

The attack by the rebels ended in catastrophic defeat at the hands of Edward's better trained men. Once the rebel attack had been defeated, Edward led his men forward to turn retreat into rout.

The Battle of Losecoat Field 1470

Welles into thinking that they were protesting against a tyrannical and unpopular king only to find that the militias of many other counties had turned out to support that same monarch. Being battered by artillery was no joke, and being encouraged to charge against steady and professional soldiers seems to have been the last straw.

So the rebels fled. As they ran they took off the surcoats of the black bull and the bear and ragged staff. They believed, perhaps with good reason, that Edward would single out men wearing such badges for retribution. The fields north toward the village of Greetham were strewn with these surcoats. And so the battle got its name of Lose Coat Field.

Edward unleashed his cavalry men to give chase, ordering them to cut down and kill any knights or lords but to show mercy to any commoners who surrendered. The pursuit went on for several miles. Sir Robert Welles and Sir Thomas of Lande were captured, Sir Richard Warren killed. Another man dressed as a knight and wearing a badge of the black bull was killed. As he fell this man let fall from his arms a small casket. The keen eyed horseman who cut him down grabbed the casket and carried it back to Edward. When it was broken open the casket was found to contain letters written to Sir Robert Welles by the Duke of Clarence. The story they revealed was remarkable, and dangerous.

Chapter 5
Aftermath

The letters found in the casket on the battlefield were politically explosive. Clarence and Warwick had been behind the uprising all along. Warwick and Clarence had been in touch with Welles from soon after the dispute that led Welles to attack Sir Thomas Burgh's house at Gainsborough. They had encouraged Welles to behave truculently, promising to give him support and aid.

The man who had been claiming to be Robin of Redesdale was, in fact, Sir John Conyers of Hornby a member of the household of Warwick. Warwick had been trying to stir up trouble elsewhere. While the places were not specified in the letters, Edward soon discovered that Lord Scrope of Bolton had raised a rebellion in Yorkshire, though few men had joined it. In the West Country the Courtney family had raised their retainers when Warwick promised to restore to them lands confiscated by Edward.

Warwick had also sent messages to other nobles and families whom he thought might have a grievance against Edward, but these men chose to stay at home and instead pass the messages on to Edward. In the days after the battle these came to Edward, making it clear that Warwick had planned to raise a combination of men who nursed grievances, kill Edward and put Clarence on the throne. And Clarence had been fully involved in the plot to kill his own brother.

Edward decided to keep private the fact that he knew Clarence and Warwick were behind the plot. Instead he sat down later that day to write in his own hand a short note to Clarence and Warwick giving them the good news of the victory he had won outside Empingham. There was, he said, no need for Warwick and Clarence to go to all the expense of keeping an army in the field, so they could disband their men and send them home. Finally, the letter said, Warwick and Clarence should come to join Edward at Grantham for a feast to celebrate the victory. The letter was sealed, then put into the hands of the envoy John Down who was given orders to deliver it in person and wait for a reply before coming back.

Down found Warwick and Clarence in Coventry, despite their promises to march to Grantham via Leicester. They told Down that they would disband their men and ride at once to Grantham with an escort of only a thousand men, just in case there were any rebels still about.

Down, Clarence and Warwick rode out of Coventry later that day. Down took the road to Stamford and expected the noblemen to take the road to Grantham, but instead they headed north toward Burton. Down called to point out the correct road, but Warwick smiled and called back that a part of their army was stationed a couple of miles north and they needed to be sent home. Down nodded and rode for Stamford.

When Edward heard that Clarence and Warwick had gone north, he leapt into action. The royal army was marched north, reaching Doncaster on 18 March. That day Edward's scouts found Warwick and Clarence in Chesterfield, marching north apparently to join Lord Scrope and his forces. Edward was blocking their route.

Edward sent a message to Clarence and Warwick promising to view them "with favour and pity, remembering the ties of blood and love and affection which had been between them". By the conventions of the day this meant that he was offering them their lives, but nothing more, in return for immediate surrender.

Edward consulted the senior nobles with him. He did not want to execute his own brother. The nobles were firm. Commoners might be excused rebellion if they had been misled into action and might escape with merely a fine, but noblemen were educated enough in the ways of politics to know what they were doing. They had no excuse, and so death was the only penalty possible. That day, 18 March, news came that Edward's youngest brother Richard Duke of Gloucester had raised the militia of the western counties and was marching north. He expected to reach Manchester on or before the 22 March.

On 19 March, Sir Robert Welles and Sir Thomas of Lande were taken to Doncaster market place and beheaded. Messengers were then sent to Clarence, Warwick and Scrope telling them that death was the penalty for rebellion, but that any non-noble who abandoned the rebellion and threw themselves on the king's mercy would be spared. As word of the message

The Battle of Losecoat Field 1470

spread through the rebel forces they began to fall apart. The men simply abandoned the rebel cause, after all many of the men had not been aware they were joining a rebellion when they had set off.

Clarence and Warwick abandoned what was left of their army on 20 March, riding with a small escort of trusted men over the Penines to evade Edward's scouts. Scrope had, in fact, already given up the struggle and surrendered to Edward before he received his letter. Edward chose not to execute him. On 24 March Edward issued a proclamation stating that if Warwick or Clarence surrendered to any royal official on or before 28 march they would still enjoy his "favour", that is their lives would be spared, but that otherwise they would be declared rebels and a reward of £1,000 would be put on their heads.

In fact Warwick and Clarence were heading south. They picked up the Duchess of Warwick and Duchess of Clarence then loaded their men on to ships in Exeter and set sail. After a piratical cruise up the Channel, capturing some Burgundian merchant ships on the way, the two fleeing noblemen landed in Honfleur and asked the King of France for asylum. Louis XI of France wanted nothing more than an opportunity to make trouble for England. He welcomed Warwick and Clarence, listened sympathetically to their tales of woe and began planning how best to use his guests to cause trouble.

The Wars of the Roses would go on.

ALSO AVAILABLE IN THIS SERIES

The Battle of Wimbledon 568
The Battle of Lincoln 1141
The Battle of Chesterfield 1266
The Battle of Northampton 1460
The Battle of Losecoat Field 1470
The Sieges of Newark 1643-46
The Siege of Leicester 1645
More to come